Dating Workbook

Mindful, authentic dating

by

Rachel New

Contents

Introduction	4
Why do I want to date?	6
What can I learn from past relationships?	9
What is my relationship blueprint?	12
What is my concept of love?	15
Who am I?	18
Do I feel good about myself?	22
Am I ready for dating?	25
What relationship skills do I need to work at?	29
What are my relationship needs?	35
What are my deal-breakers and deal-makers?	40
What kind of relationship do I want?	42
What kind of dating is best for me?	44
How does online dating work?	47
How do I write a dating profile?	49
What is the role of photos in a dating profile?	51
What kind of messages work on dating apps?	53
How do I get a first date?	56
How do I prepare for a first date?	59
Why is my date not what I expected?	63
How do I make sense of dates that don't work out?	65
How do I decide whether to have a second date?	69

How is a second date different from a first date?	71
When should I become intimate?	75
How should the first ten dates look?	78
How do I move into a relationship?	80
How do I know someone is right for me?	82
What makes a good relationship?	85
Conclusion	88
Further reading	90

Introduction

Dating in the twenty-first century can be an exciting journey where you discover things about yourself and others.

Or it can be bewildering, exhausting and heartbreaking.

Fast forward to your future self, in a great relationship. Do you want that future self to look back on your dating years with fondness or regret?

I want us to work together to make sure you don't miss out on the chance to have a great dating life – one in which you have fun, positive experiences that make you feel good about yourself. That means being equipped with self-awareness, strong relationship skills and an understanding of the psychological processes involved in contemporary dating.

From my work as a dating and relationships coach over the last five years, a background in social psychology research at the University of Oxford, training in mindfulness and life coaching, and personal experiences of successful dating and long-term relationships, I believe there are no quick fixes. Just telling you all the theory and advising you on how to avoid classic mistakes isn't going to be enough.

You're going to have to put some hard work in yourself.

That's why I've written a workbook that gets you involved rather than something you can read quickly and forget just as quickly.

Each chapter is divided into three sections:

Reflection - questions and exercises;
Discussion - key information, research and advice;
Response - follow-up tasks for you.

You'll need a notebook (or audio recording device if you prefer) for answering the questions. Find a quiet place where you won't be distracted, take your time to think about each one and treat it like a form of meditation.

You can work through the questions and exercises on your own, with a dating coach or therapist, or in a group.

You'll reflect on your previous relationships, feel good about yourself, identify your relationship needs, learn about the psychological processes behind contemporary dating, and be equipped for whatever comes your way.

This book is relevant for all genders and sexual preferences. I've used the pronoun "they" throughout. We'll cover online dating as well as other ways to meet in a range of social contexts.[1]

OK, grab your notebook and pen, and let's get started on your dating adventures!

Rachel New

---

[1] I'm based in the UK, but most research on dating has been carried out on US participants. Many of the principles of dating will apply to other cultures too: I leave it to the reader to judge how to apply each one to their particular context. Most recent research uses a range of sexual preferences for their samples, although there is still a scarcity of data from non-binary genders.

Why do I want to date?

Reflection

1. Imagine you wake up and find that you are now happily dating someone who is not only perfect for you, but also showing just the right amount of interest!

    a) How is your life different?

    b) How has this changed you?

    c) How do you feel?

    d) How does this affect the way you think and act?

2. Now imagine your life two years later. You are in a committed relationship with this person.

    a) Answer the questions again.

    b) Now compare your answers.

3. We often imagine that romance will transform our life or solve all our problems. But that depends on what you want the relationship to do. Write down your responses to each of these. You may also find it helpful to put them into order, starting with which you need most.

    a) Do you need someone to help you feel safe?

    b) Do you need someone to make you feel good about yourself?

    c) Do you need someone to understand you?

    d) Do you need someone to show off to your friends?

    e) Do you need someone to help you heal from past hurts?

    f) Do you need someone to validate your beliefs?

g) Do you need someone so your parents will stop worrying about you?

h) Do you need someone to have children with?

i) Do you need someone to challenge you and help you grow?

j) Do you need someone to provide you with financial security?

k) Do you need someone to cure you of mental illness?

l) Do you need someone you can change and improve?

m) Do you need someone you can control?

n) Do you need someone to direct your anger towards?

o) Do you need someone to blame?

p) What else do you need someone for?

Discussion

You might have thought that was a very long list, but there are probably many more. We may not even be aware of some of them. For example, we may repeatedly look for someone like one of our parents because that familiarity meets a need for security. So it might be useful to think back over previous relationships and try to identify needs we may not have been aware of.

There are also many kinds of dating experiences and relationships, some of which we will explore in this workbook. But it is important to accept that a romantic relationship can never meet all our needs, and it is not a magic bullet that can solve all our problems.

Dating and being in a relationship meet different needs. Dating can be exciting and unpredictable, meeting our needs for validation, novelty, adventure and sensation. Relationships, on the other hand, meet our needs for intimacy, security, certainty and understanding. We all need both, but at different stages in our lives one may take priority over the other. One of the aims of this workbook is to help you work out whether you're ready for a long-term relationship or still at the dating and short-term relating stage.

Response

Dating and relating work best once we've reached a certain level of self-acceptance, emotional maturity and independence. So in the next few sections, we'll reflect and work on ourselves. This is a big task that you may need more support with, but here are some starting points.

4. Begin by taking some time to reflect on how you feel about spending time on your own.

    a) Are you happy in your own company?

    b) Can you survive for an hour or two without checking for messages on your phone, both from friends/family and dating apps?

    c) Are you able to talk to yourself positively when you're feeling challenged?

    d) Do you have others you can ask for support when you need it? How easy do you find this?

5. If you find any of these hard, make it your goal to practise doing each of them over the next two weeks. Start with short periods of time, such as fifteen minutes. Make some notes on your progress and how it changes the way you see yourself.

What can I learn from past relationships?

Perhaps you are just emerging from a divorce or bereavement. Or you may have had a number of short-term relationships, but nothing serious. Perhaps you are a blank slate, ready to start dating for the first time! Whatever your history, you will need to reflect on your past relationships, of all kinds, from family to work colleagues to friends. It can be painful, but it is important to identify repeating patterns in your choices, emotions, thoughts and behaviours.

Reflection

Spend some time answering these questions in your notebook. Don't try and answer them all at once. It might take you an hour for, say, four questions.

Include family, work colleagues and friends, as well as romantic relationships. If you have no romantic relationship history, include people you've been attracted to.

1. Which of your past relationships (however short) are significant for you? Why?
2. What is your happiest memory of each?
3. What did you learn from each relationship about yourself?
4. What did you learn from them (about relationships but perhaps other things too)?
5. Were there any parts of you that were suppressed during these relationships? Did any parts flourish?
6. How were your lovers similar to each other? How were they different?
7. Why did they end? Who ended them? Looking back, do you feel at peace about the outcome for each?

8. What did you find difficult about the endings? Could they have been handled differently? Could you have ended things sooner or tried other ways to make things work?

9. Have you ever got back together with someone after breaking up? How did that work out? What can you learn from it?

10. Have you ever felt trapped in a relationship? If so, why?

11. What have you not yet come across in a lover that you would like to experience?

Discussion

It is easy to feel that you are a "failure" if a relationship didn't work out. But sometimes people aren't compatible, or they change over time and things come to a natural end. It is a very useful life skill if we can find a way to make endings as smooth as possible, and look back and remember the good things about the relationship. Endings are a part of life that we can't avoid, and our relationship needs change over time.

A relationship can be right for a particular time in our lives. There can be parts of our personalities that couldn't blossom with one person that we want to express more in the next. Perhaps your last partner was less sociable than you, or did not understand your need to play video-games to wind down from work.

We also need to hold out for someone that meets our expectations. It's easy to get into a bad relationship, not so easy to get a good one. We will think more about these issues more in the next few sections.

Response

12. Write down three ways you will do things differently in your next relationship.

13. Make a list of what you will say next time you catch yourself thinking something negative about your past, such as "I'm just no good at relationships" or "I'm never going to find love".

14. If you feel that you weren't treated well in a previous relationship, start a list of what you deserve in your next relationship. For example, "I deserve someone who communicates honestly with me".

15. Develop a short positive story about your past relationships (or your past generally) that you can use on a date. It can be hard sometimes to explain yourself without talking for too long, so it's something that needs practice!

What is my relationship blueprint?

We have an internal blueprint or template that is built up from relationships we have observed since childhood. This is like a network of ideas stored in our brain: our beliefs, values, attitudes, emotions, patterns of behaviour and so on. It tells us what is "normal" for how to behave. However, since we all have different experiences, *our* normal can be different from that of our lover!

Reflection

1. Describe a couple whose relationship you admire.
2. How did your parents/carers/other adults in your life show love to you and to each other?
3. Did they make each other happy? Was there physical affection and emotional warmth? Did they spend time together?
4. How did they argue?
5. How did they apologise, if at all?
6. How often did they praise and criticize each other and you?
7. What role did humour play?
8. What about other adult role models in your life? Go through the questions above and identify other ways of relating that have contributed to your template.
9. Do you seem to have a "type"? How does it relate to the family and other role models you've been thinking about? Is it a healthy type or one you want to break away from?
10. Were there things you "put up with" in your previous relationships that you no longer wish to?

Discussion

As a result of answering the questions above, you should now see that it is possible to become aware of your blueprint and challenge it. It can be hard work but is part of the negotiations of any new relationship. It is important to be open to new ways of doing things. We can reject someone on the basis of something that is actually very trivial, such as whether they react enthusiastically enough to the first gift you buy them!

For example, your new lover may withdraw during an argument while you like to shout and get excited. You will need to explore new ways of arguing, such as active listening, using humour to diffuse tension, not becoming defensive, and so on.[2] Your first argument can make or break the early, fragile stages of dating. So learning how to argue better before your next relationship could be something to work at now.

Communication style is another skill area where differences in your blueprint can affect the early stages of dating. One person may hold back and the other may be very honest from the beginning; or one may send messages more often than the other.

A third area of difference may be in how much effort you each put into how you dress, tidy up your home for the other's visit, or plan your dates.

> The shoe that fits one person pinches another; there is no universal recipe for living.
>
> Carl Jung, The Practice of Psychotherapy, 1966

---

[2] Read *The Seven Principles For Making Marriage Work* by John and Nan Gottman. It applies just as well to all relationships.

Try to identify when you are reacting to (a) something in your blueprint (which can be altered), or (b) something more general (that almost everyone would think is essential), such as how reliable or honest they are. Try to keep an open mind. We often begin dating with more deal-breakers than we end up with. (More about that in the section *What are my deal-breakers and deal-makers?*)

Response

11. Observe how other couples relate to each other, whether in real life, or in films or books.

12. Next time you need to disagree or be assertive with someone, try to do it differently. Later, have a debrief with them about how it went and learn from their perspective.

13. Further reading: *The Course of Love* by Alain de Botton, and *The Seven Principles For Making Marriage Work* by John and Nan Gottman.

What is my concept of love?

Reflection

1. What does being "in love" mean to you?
2. Have you ever been in love?
3. How would you characterize the difference between the emotions at the beginning of a relationship and the emotions a few years in?
4. Do you make a distinction between loving someone and being in love?
5. Did you feel loved as a child? How was that expressed?
6. How would you know if you were in love?
7. Do you want to fall in love (again)?
8. Could you be in a relationship without being in love?
9. Have you ever loved more than one person at a time? Do you believe it's possible?
10. Do you believe you are worth loving?[3]
11. Are you able to teach others how to love you?
12. Do you have the humility to learn from others about how to love them?
13. Are you able to receive love from others?

---

[3] These last four questions come from *The Art of Loving* by Eric Fromm, first published in 1956.

Discussion

People dating have a range of goals. Some are looking for love, others not. These goals will be explored more in the section *What kind of relationship do I want?* For now, let's agree that there is a range of emotional involvement in dating, and, in this chapter, focus on love.

As discussed in the previous section, we all have a blueprint or template of a loving relationship, influenced by family, friends, the media, religious faith, and art forms. But each time you fall in love, it's different. For example, you may have had a mixed experience of being in love – perhaps it was unrequited, or a manipulative or unequal relationship. Or you may now want a different kind of person than the one you had children with. You may have fallen for people quickly and deeply when you were younger, but now you are more cautious and less idealistic. You may take a longer or shorter time than the other person to express feelings or to commit. That doesn't mean their feelings are any less valid. Being with someone new means expanding your blueprints.

Your love blueprint may be too idealistic - perhaps based on the concept of a perfect God, whose love is unconditional and who can give you one hundred percent attention. Or, at the other extreme, if all your experiences of love have been abusive, you will need support in developing a new blueprint to avoid a repeating pattern.

Or you may need to recognise (and avoid) the EastEnders model of love: constantly high emotional intensity and drama, falling out and making up, and insecurity. Similarly, the chemically-induced intoxication you have at the infatuation stage are not the same as the kind of love that lasts.[4] If you have one narrow blueprint, you will find it hard to recognize other experiences of love that are equally valid. (The way love develops and changes over time in a relationship will be covered in the section *What relationship skills do I need to work at?*)

---

[4] https://sitn.hms.harvard.edu/flash/2017/love-actually-science-behind-lust-attraction-companionship

> What is love? A temporary insanity cured by marriage.
> Oscar Wilde, 1854-1900

Response

14. Explore ways in which you would be willing to adapt your blueprint. For example, is it essential to you that your lover tells you regularly that they love you? How would you feel if they don't want you to live together? How would you feel about them being friends with ex-partners? What would the role be towards any children either of you have?

15. Asking questions like "How many times have you been in love?" or "Do you believe in love?" can be good ways to make a date romantic or create some chemistry, as well as a way to find out if you're on the same page. If one is a hopeless romantic and the other a hardened cynic, things might not work out.

16. There are different ways of expressing love, including through actions, words, choices. Try the five languages of love quiz online[5] to find out which are your dominant ways of expressing love. You could ask family or friends to do it too, and then discuss the differences between you. The message from author Gary Chapman[6] is that you need to recognise another person's love languages in order to receive love from them in the way they want to express it, as well as trying to communicate with them in their love languages rather than your own.

---

[5] www.5lovelanguages.com

[6] *The 5 Love Languages: The Secret to Love That Lasts* by Dr. Gary Chapman, first published 1992.

Who am I?

Reflection

1. Ask (trusted and reliable) friends and family members how they would describe you and record their answers.

2. Add your own words – use this list to help you.

adaptable	*community-minded*	*diligent*
ambitious		*diplomatic*
analytical	*compassionate*	*direct*
articulate	*confident*	*driven*
assertive	*conscientious*	*dynamic*
attentive	*consistent*	*easy-going*
authentic	*constructive*	*efficient*
balanced	*cooperative*	*encouraging*
brave	*creative*	*energetic*
calm	*cultured*	*enterprising*
candid	*curious*	*entrepreneurial*
capable	*daring*	*ethical*
careful	*decisive*	*experienced*
cheerful	*dedicated*	*extrovert*
committed	*dependable*	*fearless*
communicative	*attention to detail*	*flexible*
	determined	

friendly	*motivated*	*productive*
genuine	*observant*	*rational*
goal-oriented	*open-minded*	*reflective*
hardworking	*optimistic*	*reliable*
high-achieving	*organized*	*resolute*
honest	*outgoing*	*resourceful*
imaginative	*passionate*	*respectful*
independent	*patient*	*responsible*
innovative	*perceptive*	*self-disciplined*
have integrity	*perfectionist*	*sociable*
introvert	*persistent*	*tactful*
inventive	*persuasive*	*tolerant*
level-headed	*positive*	*trustworthy*
loyal	*practical*	*understanding*
mature	*pragmatic*	*unique*
methodical	*precise*	*upbeat*
meticulous	*proactive*	
mindful	*problem solver*	

3. Most of these words are not appropriate for introducing yourself to potential dates (e.g. on a dating profile) and some are more important to your identity than others. However, they are useful for you becoming more confident about who you are. Pick out about ten words that you think sum up who you are, but at the same time portray you in a good light.

4. Make a list of your interests. Have recent examples of each. So if you are a hill-walker, where was your last walk? If you like films, what was the best film you saw in the last year and why?

5. What are your values – in other words, what is important to you? Use this list to help you. Use different colours to circle the most important and the fairly important.

accuracy	*decisiveness*	*friendships*	*justice*
adventure	*diversity*	*fun*	*kindness*
affection	*duty*	*generosity*	*lawfulness*
altruism	*encouragement*	*good manners*	*learning*
aesthetics	*endurance*	*gratitude*	*logic*
belonging	*equality*	*happiness*	*love*
caution	*evidence*	*harmony*	*loyalty*
career	*excitement*	*home*	*obedience*
certainty	*expertise*	*honesty*	*openness*
change	*fairness*	*humility*	*optimism*
cleanliness	*faith*	*humour*	*order*
clarity	*fame*	*imagination*	*peace of mind*
community	*family*	*individuality*	*personal*
contentment	*fitness*	*innovation*	*development*
cooperation	*forgiveness*	*integrity*	*physical*
creativity	*flexibility*	*intelligence*	*environment*
curiosity	*freedom*	*intuition*	*pleasure*

popularity	*security*	*status*	*traditional values*
recognition	*self-expression*	*style*	*truth*
resilience	*self-respect*	*success*	*wealth*
respect	*simplicity*	*teamwork*	
romance	*stability*	*tidiness*	

Discussion

Many of these questions are better discussed out loud with a coach, counsellor or some fellow daters. They are big questions that take time to think about. You can go back and add to them over time. For example, you may discover, by dating someone, that socialising regularly or getting a good work-life balance is more important to you than you realised. It's often not until you meet someone who clashes with one of your values that you realise what's important.

Being specific about your interests is important because research shows you need to be distinctive (especially on dating apps) to appeal to others. Reading in a profile that someone likes museums is very bland. Referring to a particular exhibition or floor in a museum is more authentic as well as more interesting.

Response

6. If you have an online dating profile, you could re-write it using what you have learnt about yourself, now you have a wider scope of descriptions. (You may need the help of a dating coach, and there will be more advice later in this workbook about online dating.)

7. Being clear about who you are should make you more confident in your dating. Try to see your role on a date differently: it's not just about trying to attract someone, it's about you expressing who you are and seeing if you're compatible.

Be yourself; everyone else is already taken.

Oscar Wilde, 1854-1900

Do I feel good about myself?

Reflection

1. What are the thoughts you catch yourself having about your identity and sense of self? Try to observe the beliefs and perceptions you have about yourself. For example, you might notice yourself thinking "I'm not the kind of person people fall in love with" or "I'm not a very interesting person to talk to". These beliefs will come across on dates without you even saying anything. It's important to address these, perhaps with a counsellor or coach, and explore how much truth is in them.

2. A good dating question is "What do you like about yourself?" Take time to reflect on this with reference to both your person and your physical body.

Discussion

"…so much of sex is about feeling good, not just about each other, but about your life in general"

Tom Rob Smith, *The Farm,* 2013

This is one of my favourite quotations. The same applies to how we relate to others. We need to be able to celebrate who we are – without showing off or talking about ourselves too much of course – and this is perhaps the quality that is initially most attractive to others.

Response

3. Ask your friends and family what they like or value about you. Are you surprised by their responses? Is there anything you hoped they would notice that they didn't? And were there common themes?

4. Compare these responses with your list of your values in the previous section. Are there values that express who you are that are not coming across to others? What can you do about that?
5. List up to three things about yourself that are a bit eccentric or quirky. How do you feel about these? Can you be proud of them?
6. Are there parts of yourself that you find hard to tell others about? Sometimes it can be good to talk about your vulnerabilities: mutual self-disclosure on a date has been shown to be a good thing. But we need to rehearse the "story" that we tell about them so that it is palatable and has a positive side. For example, if you have a tendency to get depressed, in the early stages of dating you might talk about what helped you to recover or how you helped others in the same situation. There is often something to be proud of in even our most challenging times. It is possible to incorporate those challenges into a positive self-image.
7. Body image is another area of self-growth for which you may need to talk to someone. Feeling good about your body can be affected by what we feed our minds with, including having friends or family that talk about their appearance too much or criticise yours. Stop watching TV, using social media, using pornography, and reading newspapers and magazines for a month and don't allow people to talk about appearance while you're with them, and see if it makes any difference to how you see yourself.
8. You may want to read *The Body Is Not an Apology: The Power of Radical Self-Love* by Sonya Renee Taylor, or investigate her website.
9. Use these positive body affirmations regularly:

    I am relaxed and comfortable in my own skin.

    My body is a temple.

    I feel good about my body.

    My body is perfect just the way it is.

    My brain is my sexiest body part.

    My body is a vessel for my awesomeness!

My body, mind and spirit are interconnected.

I am present in my body.

My body should be treated with love and respect.

I trust the wisdom of my body.

My body is a gift.

My body can be used to love others.

I love the uniqueness of my body.

Am I ready for dating?

Reflection

If you have emerged from a long-term relationship in the last two years, it's important to reflect on whether you are ready to date. Some say you should have a period of transition adjusting to being on your own and learning to be independent. Others say it can be good for the ego to do some light-hearted dating, enjoying the attention of others and having some good evenings out. (It's important to make this clear to your date so there are no misunderstandings.)

If you haven't been in a relationship for a long time, or ever, you may need to reflect on whether you are emotionally available. (More on this in the next section.)

Here are some questions to answer to see if you're ready to date again. Everyone has some fears about getting back into dating, so don't worry if your answers aren't all perfect.

1. What images spring to mind when you think about dating? Here are some possibilities:

    an exciting journey

    a hopeless task

    a complex puzzle to solve

    a terrifying trial

2. How long is it since you were emotionally involved in your last relationship? If splitting up has been a long time coming, you may be more ready to date again. But be prepared for it to open the wounds again as you allow yourself to experience emotions and vulnerability. This can be part of the healing process: it is natural to compare a new date to a previous lover, and being prepared for this can help.

3. Do you have the time and energy? Arranging and fitting dates in, as well as the mental preparation beforehand and analysis after requires mental resources. If you're doing online dating, an hour a day is thought to be what is needed to generate dates. (More about this later.)

4. Are you emotionally resilient enough right now to deal with setbacks? It is a common experience to have a good date with someone but find they don't want to see you again. There are various reasons why this happens. (More on this in the section *How do I make sense of dates that don't work out?*) It can take a while to harden yourself to the world of dating.

5. Will you be able to generate enough positive conversation or do you really need a shoulder to cry on? If it's the latter, you may find you are too "needy" for dating or be expecting too much emotional support from your dates. Friends and a counsellor may be better for this.

6. Having completed the exercises above, are you at the stage of feeling emotionally self-sufficient and good about yourself? This is what attracts people and allows you to enjoy the dating experience without getting too involved and then getting hurt.

7. Do you have a strong support network? You need a good social network of friends and family before you are ready to date. This is likely to be more helpful to your recovery than the support of a date who doesn't share history with you. So you may decide you need to focus on your friendship group first, finding ways to make new friends or re-connect with family members. Or you may decide you'll need regular input from a coach or therapist.

8. Are you using sex/dating as a way to numb the pain from your past relationship?

9. What have you learnt from my last relationship about what you want in a future relationship? It is important to have reflected sufficiently on your past relationship and future goals to know what you want from a partner.

Discussion

Research shows that daters that focused on the opportunities and gains to be had from dating (a growth mindset) saw their dating experiences much more positively than those who focused on safety and minimising hurt (a loss mindset).[7] You can train yourself to think this way, perhaps with the help of a coach.

Of course, it's possible to "overthink" the question of whether you are ready for dating. If you are having doubts, it may help to talk to a friend and think about whether you are usually a cautious or anxious person.

Do you need to change the image that comes to mind in question one? Dating can be a great way to meet new and interesting people and learn from others, even if it doesn't lead to romance – that's the growth mindset attitude.

And if you feel you ARE ready for dating, great. Keep working through this book!

Response

10. Think back to a date that you have negative memories of. Imagine yourself as a really confident, positive person describing the date to someone else. What good things can you recall? What can you laugh about? What did you learn from them? What did you like about them? What was it that was wrong for you about the other person?

11. Make a self-care plan for dating. Who are you going to talk to about your dates, before and after? Pick people who are positive, and avoid talking to people who have had bad dating experiences. What are you going to plan to do the day after a date to stop over-analysis or taking it too seriously?

---

[7] Song, S., & Lockwood, P. (2021). Frustrated or engaged? Regulatory focus predicts experiences with online dating. *Personal Relationships*.

12. If you haven't already purchased the Dating Diary[8] that accompanies this workbook, do so. It will enable you to reflect on and have a more balanced view of your dates, and learn from them.

13. Training yourself to visualise positive images of dating, and to remember what you learnt from each date and how you grew from each experience, however soon it ended.

14. Watch this video regularly before every date: shorturl.at/enpCF (or Google Rachel New "Meditate before your date" YouTube).

---

[8] To buy my Dating Diary, visit shorturl.at/mtBV8

What relationship skills do I need to work at?

Reflection

Are you one of those people who think the right relationship won't require any effort? Does the title of this section fill you with horror or fatigue? No relationship can stay in the honeymoon stage forever. Research shows that this stage (also known as the passionate stage) lasts between eighteen months and three years.[9] After that, a deeper form of love emerges (the companionate stage), or the relationship dies.

Whether your relationship can survive beyond that will to a large extent depend on your skills in relationships. Will you still get along on days when you are irritated, stressed or depressed?

Never to go on trips with anyone you do not love.

Ernest Hemingway, *A Moveable Feast,* 1964

---

1. Which of these do you need to work at? Add your own ideas too.

    a) Arguing constructively and dealing with conflict

    b) Apologising in the right way and being able to admit when you're wrong

    c) Listening sensitively without interrupting

    d) Responding appropriately when someone opens up to you

    e) Showing empathy

---

[9] Hatfield, E. (1988). Passionate and companionate love. In R. J. Sternberg & M. L. Barnes (Eds.), *The psychology of love* (pp. 191–217). Yale University Press.

f) Being open and flexible

g) Showing and talking about your feelings

h) Understanding and communicating your own needs

i) Feeling secure in a relationship

j) Being more appreciative and positive and less critical

k) Commitment and putting in the effort

l) Honesty and loyalty

m) Reliability

n) Trusting others and being trustworthy

o) Getting the right levels of time for yourself, independence and emotional involvement

p) Being consistent in your reactions and emotions

2. Now ask a close friend or family member to pick three or four you're good at and one or two they think you could improve on.

Discussion

It's not possible to address all of these in this workbook.[10] Here, one skill that all of us can work on is discussed: emotional availability.

Emotional availability is the ability to share an emotional connection. From working with clients, this model[11] was created to capture the elements of responsiveness, empathy, intimacy, openness, sensitivity, and articulation that seem to characterise people who are able to connect with others emotionally.

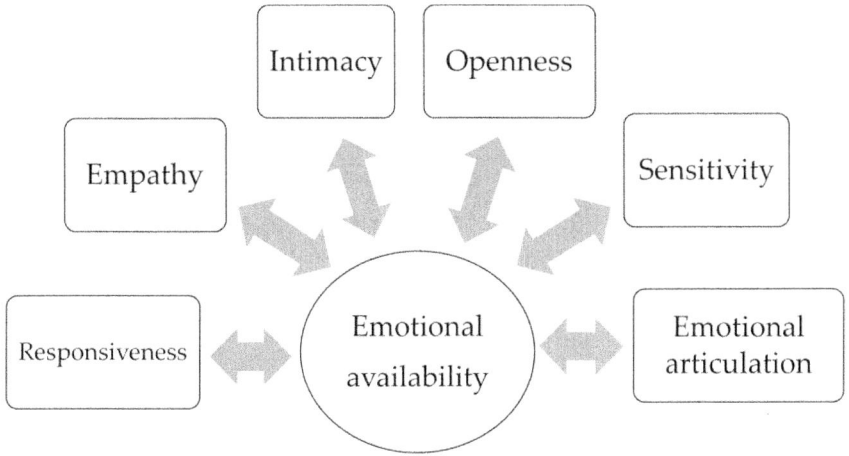

Figure 1: Model of Emotional Availability
(Rachel New, 2017)

Perhaps the question to ask is: Do others see us as warm or cold?

---

[10] For more on relationship skills, read *The Seven Principles For Making Marriage Work* by John and Nan Gottman.

[11] rachelnewdatingcoach.co.uk/2017/01/09/am-i-emotionally-available

The quality of warmth is crucial on a date. You might need to record yourself chatting with a friend on a video-chat to see how you come across. Smiling, eye contact, responding quickly and appropriately to the other person disclosing something personal, and not interrupting are some key skills that create warmth. This is perhaps the most useful area a coach can help with, as we all have our own unique way of socially interacting, and subtle changes can make all the difference.

Response

Assess yourself in these areas of emotional availability, and better still, get others to assess you:

Responsiveness:

a) What do you say when your date tells you they have recently suffered a bereavement or isn't feeling well?

b) Do you follow it up later in the conversation and the next day?

c) Are you able to find out or get a sense of how much they want to talk about their difficulty before moving onto a different topic of conversation?

d) Do you come across as warm in your facial expressions?

Empathy:

e) How do you convey that you appreciate how difficult it has been for your date to go through their divorce, or how it feels to have had a stressful day at work?

f) Are you able to use an appropriate tone of voice and non-verbal sounds and touch to convey your support and desire to understand?

g) Are you able to offer sympathy without providing solutions?

Intimacy:

h) How do you feel when your date says they can't wait to see you again, or that they have feelings for you?

i) How do your feelings change after having good sex – do you want to go straight home and be alone, or do you like to cuddle?

j) Do you feel panicky at the thought of the dating turning into something more routine, where for example you start arranging what to cook together?

Openness:

k) Are you able to talk about how you feel?

l) Do you feel comfortable with your feelings, both positive and negative?

m) Are you confident enough to say you're missing your date, or that you'd rather they didn't phone you every day?

Sensitivity:

n) Can you tell from facial expressions when your date is uncomfortable or wants you to change the subject?

o) Do you know when your date is close to tears, getting irritated, feeling offended, bored?

p) Do you know when to go home and give your date some space?

Emotional articulation:

q) Do you have the vocabulary to express a range of feelings and thoughts about your date, without having to repeat the same compliments over and over?

r) Are you able to say exactly what you like about them and give specific compliments?

s) Can you articulate feelings of physical attraction, respect and admiration, how interesting or entertaining you find them, as well as more romantic responses?

t) Are you able to ask questions that get to a deeper level?

Our emotional availability is something we can all reflect on and develop strategies to improve. We need to think about what is holding us back – have we become more cautious as a result of bad dating experiences, rejection, or previous relationship patterns? Do we need to explore a more general fear of intimacy and commitment? Or do we just need help with our social skills?

What are my relationship needs?

When we are young, we may just be grateful that someone likes us and fall into a relationship without thinking about whether they are right for us. But if you are working through this book, perhaps you realise that this is not a very good approach to finding a partner. If the starting point is knowing what you want, then you will be in a stronger position on a date and focusing on whether they are right for you rather than whether they like you.

Reflection

1. What things do you need a partner to understand about you?

2. What kind of lover do you respect?

3. Here is a list of some traits that are often important for a good relationship. Tick the ones that are especially important to you, and perhaps pick out your top ten:

   Confidence
   Reliability
   Loyalty
   Monogamy
   Emotional honesty/able to communicate feelings
   Someone with a rich inner life
   Someone with purpose, meaning, goals
   Similar politics
   Same religious beliefs
   Similar level of education/intelligence
   Someone who cares about equality and justice
   Generous
   Altruistic
   Non-judgmental
   Open-minded
   Financial security
   As busy or leisurely as me/has a good work-life balance
   Enjoys stimulating discussions
   Introvert/extrovert
   Direct/straightforward

Someone who isn't stressed/can relax easily
Someone with/without children
Someone with energy who likes physical activity
Flexible about plans
Can provide emotional support and empathy
Fun and humour
Gentle, kind, loving
Shared interests (specify)
Tactile/likes physical contact
Similar sex drive
On an even keel emotionally/not moody or volatile
Resilient
Secure and healthy self-esteem
Adventurous/likes travel
Needs space/solitude
Independent/happy for you to be independent
Needs a very close emotional connection
Likes to take things slowly
Someone you can be inspired by/admire/be proud of

Discussion

Sometimes on dating profiles there are long lists: "Don't bother contacting me if you're a, b, c, d …". This is usually a reaction against a bad past experience. This may be reasonable – such as when you are tired of explaining why Black Lives Matter yet again and only want to date people who get it. But it may be that your last bad relationship was with someone who was always playing sport and never had time for you, so you go to the other extreme and say you don't want someone sporty. It's important to think about whether our reaction against particular personality traits, behaviours or attitudes is measured.

It's also important to be confident about communicating your needs. For example, if you are the kind of person who needs a lot of solitude, you will need to discuss how often you're going to contact each other in between dates, how often you want to see each other and so on, in a way that doesn't make the other person feel like you're not interested.

Needs can be communicated in various ways. It's better to be more specific. "I need you to be more open" is much harder to respond to than "I need someone who listens to my point of view attentively without interrupting".

Sometimes we can have conflicting needs. One person might want to take things very slowly, and the other might be feeling insecure as a result. Start a conversation such as "I have this need, but I can see you have this other need, and I don't know how to balance mine against yours." If both people are feeling relaxed by this gentle and honest start-up, it should be possible to think creatively together to find a solution.

Response

Another way to think about what you want from a lover is to break it down into behaviours, emotions and cognitions (mental processes – here labelled "Mind"). Try filling in the second version of the diagram below, which is blank.

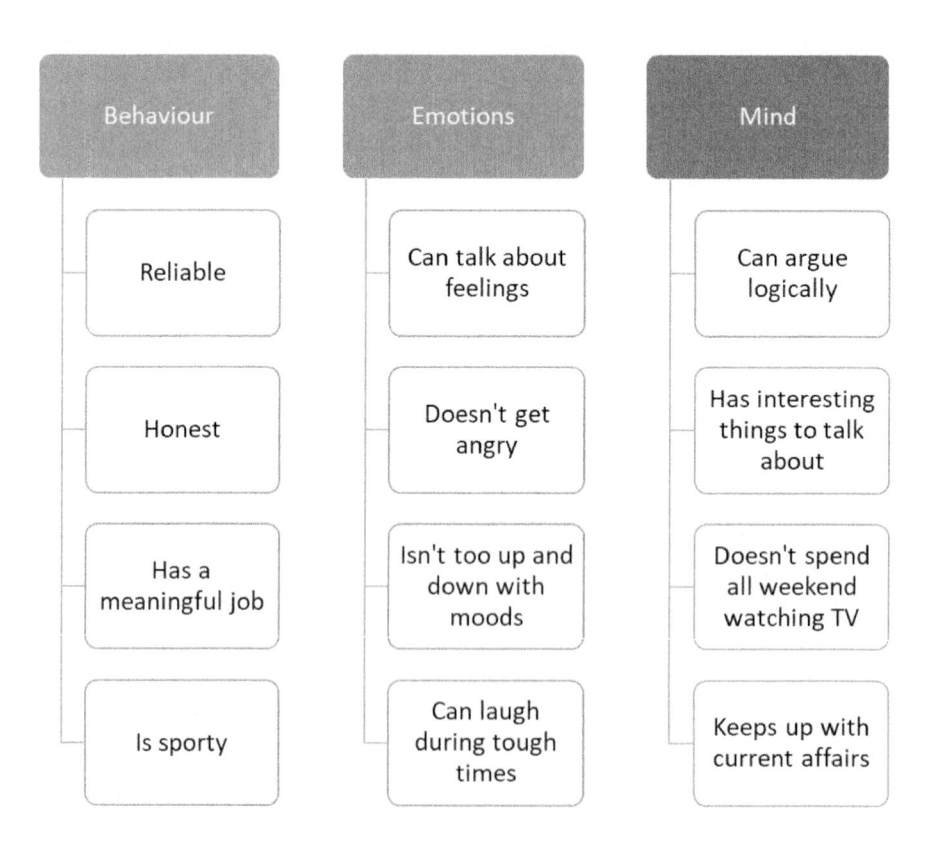

Behaviour	Emotions	Mind
Reliable	Can talk about feelings	Can argue logically
Honest	Doesn't get angry	Has interesting things to talk about
Has a meaningful job	Isn't too up and down with moods	Doesn't spend all weekend watching TV
Is sporty	Can laugh during tough times	Keeps up with current affairs

Dating Workbook   39

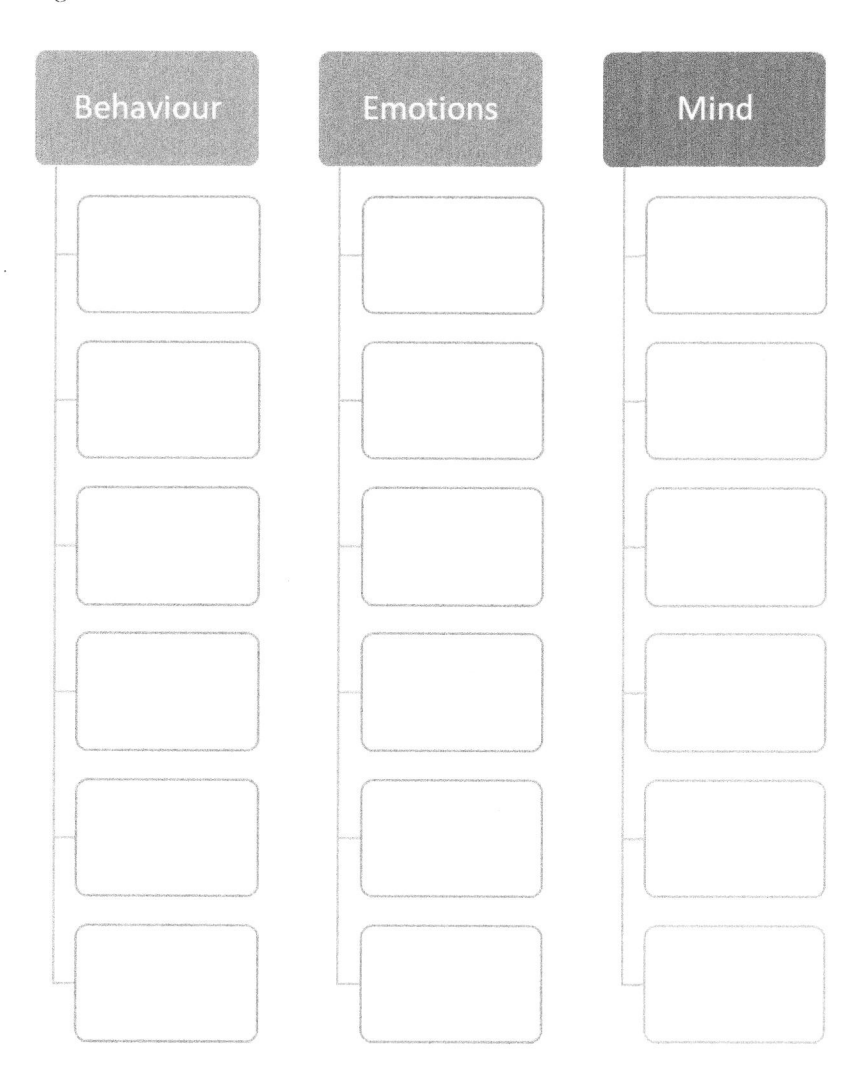

Behaviour   **Emotions**   **Mind**

What are my deal-breakers and deal-makers?

Reflection

Deal-breakers are things that you would on no account have in a relationship. Examples of deal-breakers might include smoking or living in another country.

Deal-makers are things you have to have. Examples of deal-makers might include wanting children, having been or wanting to be vaccinated against COVID, or believing in climate change.

1. Make a list of your deal-breakers and deal-makers - what you consider to be absolutely non-negotiable, rather than just desirable, in a partner. This should be a much shorter list than the list you made in the section above, on relationship needs.

Discussion

Research shows that when people go speed-dating[12] or when they think someone is interested in going on a date with them,[13] they are happy to overlook stated preferences.

This does not mean they are necessarily compatible in the long-term, but that when meeting real people face to face, we are less selective.

---

[12] Eastwick, P. W., & Finkel, E. J. (2008). Sex differences in mate preferences revisited: do people know what they initially desire in a romantic partner? *Journal of Personality and Social Psychology, 94*(2), 245.

[13] Joel, S., Teper, R., & MacDonald, G. (2014). People overestimate their willingness to reject potential romantic partners by overlooking their concern for other people. *Psychological Science, 25*(12), 2233-2240.

Only you – or your dating coach – can judge whether you are too selective, not selective enough, or just right. Being moderately selective is attractive, research shows,[14] and it is advisable to say what you're looking for in a dating profile or if asked on a date. But you don't want to rule out too many people before you start.

An example which seems too selective is a woman wanting a man who is taller than her even when she is wearing heels.[15] Is that really necessary? Imagine that someone is perfect for you in every way and you'd been searching for years for such a person. Would you really reject them because every now and then you might want to wear uncomfortable shoes for a few metres from a taxi to a party?[16]

As another example, if you have included particular ethnic or cultural backgrounds as one of your criteria, you might like to read this article.[17]

Response

2. If you have already done some dating, think back over who you have dated and whether you have broadened or narrowed down your pool of dates as time as gone on and why.

3. Ask others who are dating what their deal-breakers and deal-makers are, and why. This can help you to see that things that might seem essential to you are not to others. Once you're happy with your list, you can then explain why yours are essential to you, and feel confident about your reasons.

---

[14] Wright, R. A., & Contrada, R. J. (1986). Dating selectivity and interpersonal attraction: toward a better understanding of the elusive phenomenon. *Journal of Social and Personal Relationships, 3*(2), 131-148.

[15] I think it would be too selective for any other genders too, but this is where it is most entrenched.

[16] I owe this idea to an article by Marianne Eloise in Cosmopolitan, www.cosmopolitan.com/uk/love-sex/relationships/a34599304/short-kings

[17] rachelnewdatingcoach.co.uk/2020/09/14/can-you-help-who-youre-attracted-to

What kind of relationship do I want?

Reflection

1. At what time intervals do you think people should have sexual intimacy, call it a relationship, fall in love, move in together, and so on? What variation have you seen in these milestones in relationships of people you know?

2. What films, books, song lyrics and other art forms have influenced how you think a relationship should develop? What about real-life stories from your formative years, from how family members met their partners to how your friends formed relationships? Were these stories celebratory or did they contain a warning?

3. How did family members react when relationships broke down? How might that have influenced you?

4. How important is monogamy or exclusivity to you?

5. Do you imagine your future partner being a soul-mate who meets all your needs and shares all your dreams?

Discussion

There are many types of relationships in twenty-first century dating. It is important to clarify what you both want, and what your beliefs and values about relationships are.

In a traditional relationship both partners may keep each other close, doing most or all of their socialising together.

As people get older and have several long-term relationships under their belt, they may become more flexible and open-minded. Such people are be happy to spread their emotional support across several people, and will trust their partner to see other people they may be attracted to or have a history of intimacy with.

Some people believe it's possible to have sexual intimacy regularly without getting emotionally involved, or to be involved sexually and emotionally with more than one person.

Others want to have a long-term loving relationship without living together, with a greater level of independence.

If there are children involved, you will both have to work hard to find an arrangement that works for all of you.

You may also be open to a range of types of relationship, depending on the person you meet.

Try not to react too quickly to a model that is outside your experience.

Response

6. Make sure you know whether you are looking for something short or long term. If you're new to dating, it's unlikely that you'll meet the perfect partner straightaway. You are most likely to have a few short-term experiences first. But you might decide you definitely don't want something casual, and that you want there to be some emotional involvement. It's a question that should get asked on the first or second date, to avoid misunderstandings.

7. Decide in advance whether or not you are willing to try a "no strings attached" relationship. Some people find they can achieve the emotional detachment needed, but many don't. You may have to learn the hard way. But it's best to decide in advance, not AFTER you've started falling for someone.

8. How would you feel about your new partner meeting up with ex-partners or seeing friends they could be attracted to?

9. For an example of a couple living in different homes, read *Astonishing Splashes of Colour* by Clare Morrall.

What kind of dating is best for me?

Reflection

1. How have you met people in the past? What is good and bad about each? Have you noticed any differences in your experiences of each?

    (a) general online dating apps

    (b) specialist/niche dating apps for specific interest/hobbies/needs

    (c) matchmaking agencies

    (d) meeting through friends and family

    (e) meeting at work

    (f) meeting through hobbies, classes, voluntary work, and social events

    (g) meeting on social media

    (h) speed dating

2. Which of the above would you like to try? Which would you like to do more or less of? What is a good balance for you?

3. How long do you wait before suggesting a first date? Or, if you prefer the other person to make the first move, why?

4. Do you prefer to arrange lots of first dates or wait for one you feel a strong connection with? How many dates would you want in a month?

5. How often do your first dates lead to second dates?

6. When dates don't work out, is that you or them making the decision? Are you happy with your level of "pickiness"?

7. How quickly do you get involved emotionally or sexually? Is this something you are flexible about? Do your emotions develop at a similar rate to the other person's?

8. How much communication do you like in between dates?

9. At what point would you expect exclusivity when dating someone?

10. If an early date leads to sexual intimacy, would you expect to spend the night together? How would you communicate if you didn't want to see the other person again after intimacy?

Discussion

If you haven't dated for a long time, you will find that the unwritten rules of dating have changed. People may end things by text message, communicate less in between dates and be more distant emotionally for longer. It's a good idea to discuss these things openly with your date. For example, if your date asks if you'd like to come back to their home, saying "yes" does not imply consent to intimacy, but make sure you're clear if you are not yet decided about whether you'd like to become intimate. Don't assume they would want you to stay the night – make sure you have the means to get home if necessary, and ask "So what normally happens now? Do I get a cab home?" and then if they want you to stay, they will say so. If you stay the night, don't stay too long in the morning – have something planned that you have to get back for so it's not awkward.

Response

11. Dating norms vary between ages, cultures, and over time, so it is not possible to provide prescriptive advice here. The purpose of this section is for you to know what you feel comfortable with. You may need to ask friends or search online for local norms, but remember you can reject those norms!

12. Make a plan for your dating over the next three months. How many people are you going to message each week; how many first dates do you want; can you book a speed dating session or join an evening class or something else?

13. Can you organise your own social event for local single people, such as a walk, book club, picnic or drinks? What other local organisations could help to host or publicise your event, such as a library, pub, bookshop or café?

How does online dating work?

Reflection

These questions are best discussed with a dating coach, as there is research on what works best. But it is also good for you to think about your own preferences, maybe in discussion with other daters. When you are new to dating, what seems normal to you may convey messages to more seasoned daters that you are unaware of. For example, it may come naturally to you to send lots of messages every day when you start dating someone. But this will probably come across as too keen to a more experienced dater.

1. How long should you message for before arranging a date?

2. Should you swap phone numbers before arranging a first date?

3. Where should you have the first date?

4. Are any topics that you wouldn't want to discuss on a first date?

5. Is it OK to give a compliment about appearance on a first date?

6. Should you keep messaging after setting up the first date?

7. Should you kiss on a first date? How do you work out if your date wants to be kissed? Is it safe to kiss? Is it OK to ask if your date has been vaccinated/recently tested?

8. How soon would you message someone after a first date? What should you say?

9. How often do you like to message someone in the first few weeks of dating?

10. What is the longest length of time it would be polite to leave before texting back?

11. Should you plan the next date during the date/immediately after?

12. How soon would you want to be sexually intimate? What are the current government guidelines regarding COVID in your country on sexual intimacy when you are not in a long-term relationship?

13. How would you end things?

Discussion

With all these issues, each dater will have their own history and trigger points. They may have recently experienced someone being too clingy or too distant and be reacting against that. They may interpret your behaviour as being more interested than you are, or the opposite. So it's important to openly discuss questions like "How often do you like to communicate between dates?" or "Do you like to kiss at the end of a first date?" rather than trying to guess what they want. Most misunderstandings in the early stages of dating arise from one party forming assumptions about the other! Post-pandemic, it can become more acceptable to express what we feel comfortable with, especially around physical closeness.

Response

Experiment with different levels of open communication on your dates or when messaging and see what kind of response you get. Many people are relieved to get these things out in the open, and even if things don't work out, you can learn a lot about the range of priorities, goals, values and preferences daters can have – if you're prepared to listen. This will stop you projecting your own ways of doing things onto others, and make you more open to relating in new ways.

How do I write a dating profile?

Reflection

1. Read other profiles first and see what you find engaging and what is cringe-worthy/boring/done too much etc.

2. Think about the kind of person you want to attract. (Look back at your notes from the section on deal-breakers and deal-makers.) Now ask yourself: What kind of profile will they be attracted to?

Discussion

Many daters find writing a dating profile very difficult. It's not the same as a CV but it is in some ways you advertising yourself: it's where the personal becomes public. It's important to protect your identity (against identity fraud or online crime, for example) by not giving any identifying information such as surname, exact location or job title. But you want to come across as a human being that the person reading your profile can imagine going on a date with. It's a fine balance, and something many daters get professional help with.

Response

3. If you already have profiles on dating apps, make alterations based on what you discovered in the first two tasks. If you don't have one, you will need to register with an app first to see what kind of profile you can have as each app is different. Many give prompts for you to complete, such as these from Bumble: "If I had three wishes …" or "When no one's watching I …" (To get help with which apps to use, talk to a dating coach, as this information varies for different relationship goals, ages, cultures and locations.)

4. Here are a few more tips for a good profile:

    a) Be specific – don't say "I like visiting art galleries", describe an exhibition you'd like to visit or have recently visited.

    b) Keep it short.

c) Be funny and light-hearted.

d) Check grammar and spelling very carefully.

e) Use informal language - be chatty, not CV-style.

f) Come across as warm, human, authentic, imperfect.

g) Convey positive emotions.

h) Use positive words not negative ones.

What is the role of photos in a dating profile?

Reflection

1. Have a look through some dating profiles online. Look at the photos but also the written profiles. Do you see any correlation between the two? What can you deduce from photos about personality, values, social status, education, goals, mental health, emotional intelligence?

2. What attracts you about (a) the context and (b) the physical appearance?

Discussion

It is very easy to be superficial on dating apps, looking only at the photos and not the written profiles. Unconscious bias can be at work, making us more likely to "like" or "swipe right" on people who are "like us", whether that's based on ethnicity, class, dress sense, love of animals, or whatever. But dating is partly about allowing ourselves to date outside our comfort zone, broadening our horizons and learning new perspectives.[18] So make the effort not to draw too many conclusions from other people's photos. From the above tasks, you probably realised that there isn't much of a connection between photos and who the person really is. Unless you want to avoid dog lovers, gun owners or football fanatics, the photos can be misleading.

When it comes to *your* profile, however, you'll need to accept that others are likely to be judging you quickly and superficially.

Response

Plan some occasions for taking new photos. Here are some tips:

a) Only use high quality photos and crop or edit if necessary

---

[18] rachelnewdatingcoach.co.uk/2020/10/07/can-dating-change-the-world

b) Have an interesting or brightly coloured background

c) Pictures need to be in context, not your bathroom - a café or outdoor scene is best

d) No animals or football (unless they are essential shared interests)

e) No beer glasses or drunken pub shots

f) No exes or children

g) No mess - the eye is drawn towards objects that don't need to be there, like a kitchen cloth, a dirty cup, a pile of newspapers etc

h) If you use a picture with your friends, make sure there is an arrow pointing to which one is you

i) Look slightly mysterious - don't grin inanely

j) Look classy - don't wear your football shirt

k) Iron your clothes - your collar should be sharp if you have one

l) Only have one photo with sunglasses

m) Make sure your face can be seen when viewed on a mobile phone

n) Have one full length photo

o) Photos must be recent

p) Your face at an angle is more interesting than straight on

q) Don't make it too feminine/flowery unless you want to attract a flowery person

r) Don't reveal too much flesh – it's too early for that!

What kind of messages work on dating apps?

Reflection

1. What is your immediate response to the thought of spending time each evening messaging strangers? Do you have previous experience of this? What are your hopes and fears for messaging on dating apps?

2. How does this compare with your messaging behaviour to family and friends – is it similar or different? If it's different, why?

3. How many messages would you expect to exchange with someone before arranging a date?

4. How would you feel if the other person asked you for a date before you were ready? And what if they weren't ready when you asked them?

Discussion

Messaging brings out real personality differences. Some daters hate it, others don't want to do anything else. When you first start dating, you may need to message for longer before you feel ready to arrange a date. But don't read too much into it if the other person wants a date in a shorter or longer time than you. It's a product of their previous experiences as well as their personality, and doesn't tell you much about whether you're compatible. After all, hopefully messaging isn't something you'll be doing too much of once you're in a committed relationship.

You may be questioned about things that you find intrusive before meeting. Often this is just a difference in experiences or personality. Some people are more open than others, more used to communicating electronically, or want the process to be more efficient. They may have had bad experiences with previous daters and want to make sure you are not like them in some specific way. Perhaps their previous date or partner was desperate to have children (and they don't) or drank too much. They may ask you questions to make sure you are not like that. What underlies their questions will be discussed in the next section.

Some of you may have heard horror stories from friends or the media about inappropriate messaging. That is something that can largely be avoided with the right profile and photos. Your choice of app is another factor. Some apps are better than others at allowing you to report and block people and what action they take against them. A dating coach can provide the latest information about which apps are best.

Another dimension to receiving unwanted messages is racism. Many ethnic minorities experience this and may choose to use dating apps that are specifically for particular ethnic groups, or ones with ethnic filters (which have advantages and disadvantages when it comes to reducing racism).[19] Again, some apps are better than others at dealing with this, and at using data about political affiliation to calculate compatibility between users, so that you can avoid people with particular viewpoints.

Response

Here are some tips for effective messages. It can be a useful exercise to go back through your messages on dating apps, and see if you can identify anywhere you could have improved the messaging. (This doesn't mean the messaging is what caused things not to work out. But it's a good source of data to help you identify concrete examples.)

- Less is more: a very short question is more stylish and snappy.
- Correct spelling and grammar are deal-breakers for many daters, especially women.
- Don't say "sorry" or "please".
- Don't refer to their appearance or sexual attraction.
- Use words like "fascinating", "cool", "I'm intrigued by", "I'm curious about …".
- Refer to specific things from profile and ask questions.

---

[19] rachelnew.medium.com/dating-apps-could-do-more-to-combat-racism-c9d6ed66326e

- Show, don't tell. For example, don't say you like humour. Show it by being funny and laughing at their jokes. (Research shows that using emojis helps.[20])
- Show warmth and empathy.
- Don't ask predictable questions like "How was your day?"
- Save your most interesting conversation for when you meet.
- Check crucial things before you meet e.g. smoking, whether they have children, where they live, are they actually single, what kind of relationship or dating experience are they looking for.

In love there are two things—bodies and words."
Joyce Carol Oates, 1938-

---

[20] Gesselman, A. N., Ta, V. P., & Garcia, J. R. (2019). Worth a thousand interpersonal words: Emoji as affective signals for relationship-oriented digital communication. *PloS One, 14*(8), e0221297.

How do I get a first date?

Reflection

Your messaging should enable them to imagine what it would be like on a date with you.
1. Write down some words to describe such a date.
2. Pick the one most important word.
3. Now write down words to describe how you both should feel on the date.

Discussion

Perhaps the most important words to describe a good date are around the ideas of feeling safe, understood and at ease with yourself. How does this compare with your list? Are these important to you?

The most important part of dating coaching is facilitating this experience for both parties. This will be addressed in the next section. But first the messaging must enable them to imagine a date with you where they feel safe, understood and at ease (with themselves and you).

In the previous section, the possibility of being asked questions that seem to you intrusive or unusual. This is often because the other person wants to feel safe, understood and at ease. Try to work out what it is they really want reassurance about if you don't feel comfortable asking; or ask "Why do you want to know that?" or say "I feel like this is something best discussed in person – it's quite personal!"

You, in turn, must make sure they pass the same tests. If you feel uneasy or unsure of whether you trust them, talk to a dating coach or a friend experienced in dating. It may be that you are mistrusting everyone after a bad experience or are generally a person who finds it hard to trust. Or it may be that you have good judgement in this area and can pick up the red flags. Never go on a first date with someone if you have reservations about your safety. More on this in the section *How is a second date different from a first date?*

Response

Below are some of the best ways to refine your messaging so that you are conveying these ideas of trust, safety and ease. However, this is best done working with a dating coach who can look at real messages you have sent and received and give you specific feedback in context.

4. Try to create a sense of warmth. This can be emotional or physical warmth – both will have an effect, enabling them to trust you and to feel safe.

    a) For emotional warmth, talk about your own positive emotions. You could say "I'm feeling really optimistic about …" or "I'm so motivated by …" or "I feel really relaxed about …". Avoid negative emotions.

    b) If it's winter, you could say "So let's talk about this more when we're sitting by a cosy fire in a country pub!".

    c) If it's summer, "Would love to be having a stroll along the beach in the evening sun right now. How far are you from the beach?!"

    d) It's good to make a few jokes about possible dates before broaching the subject of an actual date, to help you both get used to the idea and imagine it. Some daters are more nervous than others about the first date and need this thinking time.

    e) Using smiling emojis instead of exclamation marks can convey a sense of both warmth and light-heartedness.

5. Acknowledge an unspoken need for reassurance about safety. If you've chosen a pub for a date, tell them that it's only a few minutes' walk from the train station along a well-lit main road.

6. Don't message back and forth too much after the initial conversation. Move onto arranging a date after roughly ten messages each.

7. If there is a good topic of conversation going on, you can ask "Why don't we continue this conversation over a drink/coffee?".

8. Be confident. For example, ask *where* they'd like to meet rather than *if* they'd like to meet . You could say something like "We should probably go on a date soon".

9. Suggest some interesting places to meet: do some research and find some fun or unusual activities, or just make them up as part of some light-hearted banter. Even if you don't use them for a first date, it can be fun to discuss them!

10. Sometimes finding a time when you can meet can involve a lot of messaging. Try to keep it as simple as possible to avoid killing off the spark! A first date is best kept simple and short: a walk and a coffee; or early evening drinks in a quiet bar.

11. At this point, many daters will swap phone numbers to make it easier to communicate. But many others will prefer not to do this, for reasons of privacy. Since most first dates don't lead to second dates, this is wise.

12. Don't continue messaging after the date is arranged. This will keep the momentum going more than messaging without a purpose. Message again the day before to confirm. Be aware that many daters have experienced ghosting at this point: not getting any reply at all. Many people on dating apps have never been on a date, are very new and scared, suffer from social anxiety, or realise they're not ready to date. They may have a reality check after the practicalities of arranging the date and decide they can't do it. In this case, some will make an excuse but most will bury their heads in the sand and ignore your messages, hoping you will go away. This is a sign of emotional immaturity or an inability to manage conflict. Dating apps do not make people accountable for their actions (unless they are banned for e.g. abusive or inappropriate communication) and so they are never confronted with this pattern of behaviour. Don't blame yourself. Accept that this happens and plan an alternative evening for yourself just in case.

How do I prepare for a first date?

Reflection

What you will need to decide:

1. What do you hope to achieve on a first date? What do you want to find out?

2. Where will you meet?

3. How long should the date last?

4. What should you wear?

5. Who should pay?

6. What should we talk about? What shouldn't we talk about?

Discussion

When people first start dating, they often go for drinks or a meal on a first date, but as they become more seasoned, they may move to daytime coffee dates or after-work drinks. This is because they know that most first dates don't lead to second dates, and they don't want to waste time and money. You can artificially create romance and a strong connection with a lot of people with the right atmosphere and a few drinks, but that doesn't tell you anything about compatibility. It's a better test if you get on well over an hour long date in daylight. Think of the first date like a long speed dating encounter: it's more for screening out the majority of people you aren't right for. As video-dates become more popular, this is changing to some extent as the video-date takes over that role, but the first face-to-face date is still an important test of the basics.

Keeping it short is good because you need to reflect on how things went, away from the person. This is where the use of a dating diary[21] is useful, to reflect on how things went and to what extent the date meets

---

[21] To buy my Dating Diary, visit shorturl.at/mtBV8

your list of requirements. Your judgment is even more biased than usual when you're on the date, and you will tend to forgive and ignore what doesn't fit. An hour to ninety minutes is fine for a first date. Never discuss whether to go on a second date while on the first date. You need time to reflect and observe your feelings as well as the cold, hard facts of compatibility.

Once you've decided on a rough location and time for your date, you might like to do some research. If you pick an area with only one café and it's full, what's your back-up plan? If you're going to a pub, do you need to book? Is it important to either of you that the pub is quiet and not too crowded? Check for recommendations and reviews or ask for recommendations from local social media groups. If you are regularly dating in a particular town or city, start making lists of good places to go and try them out in advance if possible.

Next, think about what you're going to wear. Ask friends or your dating coach for their reactions to particular outfits. What you wear will vary according to your date activity, time of day, what you feel comfortable in and how you want to portray yourself. Make sure it's very clean and uncreased. Clean and polish footwear; check carefully in the mirror for stains and holes!

It's probably best to be fairly casual rather than too formal. Unless you're going to a smart/expensive place, it's a good idea to not have formal footwear AND clothes. For example, those who tend towards feminine attire might want to pair a smart top with flat boots or shoes; the more masculine can wear a shirt with a collar paired with jeans and boots or shoes. Trainers that are shiny/sparkly (for the feminine look) or leather brown/black (for the masculine look) are also a good way to get balance between smart and casual.

Make sure there isn't a big discrepancy between what you're wearing in your profile photos and what you wear on the date. For example, if you are dressed up to the nines in your photos it might be a disappointment when you turn up in a sweatshirt and no make-up. This might be interpreted as you not making an effort when you clearly do on other occasions.

On the other hand, a lot of make-up can be interpreted in various ways: some people find it intimidating, others may feel you're portraying an artificial version or yourself or that you're not comfortable with your unadorned appearance; still others will see you as creative and proud of who you are. So this isn't an argument for not wearing it, but it's good to be aware of how it might be perceived.

Remember that when people don't know much about you, they overinterpret features that stand out. So if their strongest memory of you after the date is your make-up, that's what they will use to make a judgment about whether they want to see you again. Ideally, your make-up level shouldn't be very different from how you are in your profile pictures so your date knows what to expect.

The bill should be split. Both parties should offer to do so. This is another reason for not going out for dinner or expensive drinks! Don't feel embarrassed about saying early on in the date something like "Just checking you're happy that we'll split the bill at the end? That's what I normally do" so there is no misunderstanding. If someone isn't happy with that, maybe they're not right for you. If something is being booked before the date, check during the messaging that they will reimburse you. You wouldn't feel bad about doing this with a friend, so why should you with a stranger?

Prepare for the conversation. Have some questions you can ask about them from their profile, and purchase 150 dating questions[22] or find some online to choose from. There should be a mix of light-hearted and a bit more searching. Practise following up their answers with another question to develop the topic further. The purpose of the conversation is not for you to impress them but to find out if there is any compatibility. This skill is something a dating coach can work extensively with you on: the quality of conversation is one of the most significant factors in why first dates don't turn into second dates.

---

[22] To buy my dating questions, visit rachelnewdatingcoach.co.uk/purchase

Response

Now look back at your answers in the reflection section and decide what you need to work on. Set aside time to go through your wardrobe, try out new venues for dates, or practise your conversation skills.

Why is my date not what I expected?

Reflection

1. Have you had dates where the person did not look like their photos or you weren't attracted to them in person? Perhaps their voice was surprising or they didn't smell right? Did you spend most of the date trying to reconcile the person you had imagined and the reality?

2. Have you found yourself developing feelings for someone before you have even met?

Discussion

The technical term for this disappointment is expectancy violation.[23] We build up a picture of what we think the other person is like, filling in the gaps in ways that are projections of our ideal date. So we may give them a deep voice, a quick-witted sense of humour and empathy even when there is no evidence of these.

Your date can take their time to curate the perfect answer – but in real life, be much slower to create that repartee.[24]

The longer we message, the more complex our imaginary date. So the discrepancy becomes greater. We may develop an emotional bond with this imagined person, especially if we message a lot or message when we are feeling lonely or emotional.

This means it is better to arrange the date earlier on and to be disciplined about our involvement.

---

[23] Frost, J. H., Chance, Z., Norton M. I., & Ariely, D. (2008). People are experience goods: Improving online dating with virtual dates. *Journal of Interactive Marketing, 22*, 51–61.

[24] Whitty, M. T. (2008). Revealing the 'real' me, searching for the 'actual' you: Presentations of self on an internet dating site. *Computers in Human Behavior, 24*(4), 1707-1723.

What we are attracted to in an online profile is not the same as what we are attracted to in real life.[25] It is almost impossible to predict compatibility from the kind of characteristics that can be searched for in a profile. Experiential attributes (such as humour and warmth) are much more important. The unique interaction between two people is not something that the algorithms on dating apps can yet capture.[26]

Reflection

3. Read *The Heartfix* by Stella Gray, 2016, for a true life account of how easy it is to fall in love without even meeting.

4. Try a video-date before meeting face to face, to eliminate some of the discrepancy.

5. Keep referring back to your list of deal-breakers and deal-makers during the messaging period. What do you need to find out before you meet?

6. Avoid emotional and sexual intimacy before you meet.

---

[25] Wotipka, C. D., & High, A. C. (2016). An idealized self or the real me? Predicting attraction to online dating profiles using selective self-presentation and warranting. *Communication Monographs, 83*(3), 281-302.

[26] Joel, S., Eastwick, P. W., & Finkel, E. J. (2017). Is romantic desire predictable? Machine learning applied to initial romantic attraction. *Psychological Science, 28*(10), 1478-1489.

How do I make sense of dates that don't work out?

Reflection

1. Can you recall a date that you thought went really well but, inexplicably, your date wasn't interested in meeting again. What did you tell yourself after?

2. Now think about a friend telling you about a similar scenario happening to them. How did you help them make sense of it?

3. What do you consider the aim or aims of a date?

Discussion

In the first scenario, did you say any of these:

"I'm just no good at dating!"

"I'm never going to meet someone!"

"No one ever wants a second date with me!"

"There's something wrong with me!"

And in the second, did you say anything like these:

"Don't worry, it'll happen for you one of these days!"

"There's nothing wrong with you. It's their loss!"

"Maybe they just weren't ready for a relationship?"

"They weren't the one for you."

"It just wasn't meant to be."

"The timing wasn't right. Maybe they had been hurt or just come out of a long-term relationship, or need to focus on their career right now?"

When something goes wrong, we often blame ourselves, but when it's someone else, we find other reasons. Why can't we reassure ourselves like we would a friend?

We can. We just need to train ourselves.

The technical terms for these two phenomena are **dispositional attribution** and **situational attribution**.

Dispositional attribution is a term for the way we tend to attribute our own "failure" to internal factors - ourselves, our personality (disposition) and our talents.

Situational attribution is where we explain the failure of *others* in terms of external factors, like the situation or other people.

"Failure" isn't the right word to use here in any case. Just because a date doesn't lead to another date, it doesn't mean it's a failure. First of all, it depends on what your aim for the date was. Look back at your answer to question 3. Did you say your aim was to find a relationship? If so, you might want to edit that. Finding the *right* relationship for you might be better. Then letting go of the possibility of having a relationship with the *wrong* person actually *supports* your aim!

Imagine you are out shopping for a new shirt. You have to look through lots of shirts that you don't want before you find the right shirt. You know that is a necessary part of the process. The point at which it becomes tedious varies from person to person, but you at least accept that the sifting process is unavoidable. Rejecting a shirt does not mean you have "failed".

The same sifting process is essential in dating. You can decide a person isn't right for you, and so can they. Sometimes they may reach that realisation before you. That *can* feel less empowering than being the one to say "I don't think we're right for each other" but it doesn't have to. Maybe you will be the decision-maker next time.

But what about that date that seemed so perfect? It had romance, that sense of shared reality, plans for future dates, that meeting of souls? You were so confident but then they went silent on you. This is a very common scenario, with lots of possible explanations.

Mostly, it will be random reasons that you will never know about. Don't look for an answer when you don't have the data. Maybe their Dad died, maybe they met the person of their dreams the next day, maybe their ex got in touch, maybe they got made redundant at work. You are not important in their lives right now, and so significant events can easily overwhelm the memory of one short date.

Or it could be because your date is not ready for a relationship. They may be very skilled at making you feel special, telling you they've never felt this strong a connection before, creating the impression that you are the most interesting and attractive person in the world. Or you may share lots of values and experiences or be good at making each other laugh and feel at ease. These can be the ingredients for the perfect date.

But the ingredients for the perfect date are not the same as the ingredients for a relationship. Many people can't sustain this level of attentiveness, and they know it. So they are scared that if they see you again they'll blow it. Rather than take the risk, they simply stop messaging you. It's a cowardly way out, but it doesn't mean your perfect date was imagined. It just means it can't be repeated.

In fact, the more wonderful the experience, the more someone can be scared off. A really good date can make the prospect of intimacy very real. "Wow, I can actually imagine being in a relationship with this person!" they may think. But if they are not in a position to commit to a relationship right now, they may decide not to mess you around. Perhaps they know deep down that they don't have the time or energy, or haven't fully moved on from a previous relationship. They don't know any other way to behave on a date than to act the part of someone that is ready for intimacy but they know they can't keep doing that.

Of course, that isn't an excuse for not telling you nicely, "I'm really sorry, I loved our date and you are great, but I now realise I'm not in a position to get involved right now." But it can explain rather than excuse their behaviour, and that can help you not to take it to heart.

Response

Make a list of what to tell yourself next time this happens and use it. Include a list of what you like about yourself and can offer a relationship. If you feel good about yourself beforehand, you can protect yourself from being damaged by this. Not everyone is affected by this behaviour to the same extent. Focus on feeling sorry for them and their limited relationship skills instead.

You can take steps to reduce the chances of this happening by talking on the date about how you like to be treated after a date. Say things like "Ghosting isn't something I experience much I think because I give off the right vibe that I don't want to be treated like that" or "I really like it when someone has the courage to tell me straight if they don't want to date me again".

You can make sure you are the one to message after the date. It's not their job to chase you and you are both equally responsible for following up. Wait about twelve to twenty-four hours after the end of the date. If you want another date, say something like "Great to meet you and hope you got home OK. Would love to meet up again. I'm thinking of going to that art exhibition I mentioned if you'd like to come along?"

If you haven't heard back within, say, forty-eight hours. you can message something like "OK, as I haven't heard from you I guess you don't want to meet again. Bit disappointed that you didn't feel able to tell me, but wishing you all the best for your dating!" Often, this will get a reply and an apology!

On the other hand, there are many wonderful, decent people out there who think it's quite ok to just not message after the date as a way of gently and quietly communicating that the one date was enough. Like a dignified silence when you disagree with someone but don't want to get into an argument, the post-date silence in itself is a message, and it doesn't have to be interpreted as being cruel, thoughtless or selfish.

How do I decide whether to have a second date?

Reflection

Do you have any memories of dating where you wished you'd ended things earlier? If so, what were the reasons? And when did those reasons first display themselves? Could you have picked up on them earlier?

Look back at your deal-breakers list from an earlier section. Have there been any times when you've ignored these and continued dating someone? What happened?

If you've just been on a first date, complete an entry in your dating diary[27] if you have one; or make notes on what you found out about the other person, what you found attractive and what you have reservations about.

Sit for a while and listen to your emotions and your physical sensations. How do you feel about the date, the person and the prospect of seeing them again?

Discussion

When you first start dating, you may say "yes" to lots of second dates, when looking back, you can see the person wasn't right for you. This is good experience, but you may get to a point where you become more brutal and are more selective about who you have a second date with.

We often brush under the carpet what later become red flags. We may be forgiving of personality traits, values or ways of life that we realise later just aren't going to work in the long-term.

---

[27] To buy my Dating Diary, visit shorturl.at/mtBV8

For short-term dating experiences – up to three months, say – these issues might not matter too much. It can be good for us to see other ways of living, behaving and seeing the world. The more experience we have, the better we will get at judging what we really need.

"The meeting of two personalities is like the contact of two chemical substances: if there is any reaction, both are transformed."
Carl Gustav Jung, *Modern Man in Search of a Soul*, 1933

But for long-term relationships, we may decide that there are some things that just aren't going to work for us. So if you want your dating to be more efficient, you need to be objective (use your list of deal-breakers) as well as intuitive.

Response

Don't decide on the date whether you want another date. Develop some standard ways of ending a date that don't commit you.

If you're not sure and need time to think, or even if you feel sure at the time, say something like "Thanks for a great time! Let me know what you think of that film!" or "It was great getting to know you!" or "Really glad we met up!"

If you're quite sure you *don't* want to see them again, say something like "Thanks for a great time! Let me know if you ever watch that film!" or "Good luck with the dating!" or "Great to meet you – maybe we'll bump into each other at a singles night!"

How is a second date different from a first date?

Reflection

1. Think back over any second dates you've had and how they were different from the first dates. Did the conversation develop or deepen? Did you do different things? Was there more intimacy? Did you discover surprising new things about them?

2. What do you think the purpose of a second date is, compared with a first date? (To help you, look back at your answer to the purpose of a first date in the section about preparing for a first date. You could also think about the difference between a first and second interview for a job, where there are two stages in a recruitment process. What is achieved at each stage?)

Discussion

A first date should establish whether you feel comfortable with someone and some basic information about what you have in common. The conversation should be fairly easy and relaxed, you should be able to make each other laugh, and you should have an idea of what is important to them or interests them. You should have found out information relevant to your essential deal-breakers. These might be their current relationship status (e.g. making sure they are single), smoking behaviour, wanting/having children and other caring responsibilities, their occupation and living arrangements, and where they live.

Many people make the mistake of thinking that a second date should be very similar to a first date, and are just relieved everything is going well. Although this can be enjoyable, it won't leave either of you feeling a sense of satisfaction or moving forward after the date. Highest rated dates are ones where a deep connection was made, topics of conversation were about meaning and purpose, and there was mutual self-disclosure.[28] You need to get your date down to a deeper level.

On a second date, people may reveal physical or mental health challenges and some information about their relationship history. (It is important to prepare a positive story about your own relationship history that enables you to provide enough but not too much information. This was covered in the section about your relationship history.)

It is very important to find out what kind of relationship they want and how they see that in practice. For example, you can ask how they want a new relationship to be different from their last. This will reveal a lot about their attitudes towards and expectations for relationships. Or you can ask "What do you need me to understand about you?". This should open up a much deeper level of vulnerability and disclosure. If they are unwilling to open up about themselves, this also tells you a lot about them. It may indicate a problem such as communication difficulties, emotional maturity or self-awareness.

If you intend to pursue a sexual relationship or a casual no-strings relationship, there are a number of other issues you will need to check. Questions about sexual intimacy will be covered in the next section.

You also need to be on the alert for red flags. (See list below.) Part of this is finding out more about their day-to-day life, their family relationships, their regular commitments, what they feel strongly about, and their attitudes and beliefs. But you will find out more if you ask indirect questions. For example, rather than asking "What are your attitudes towards women?" you could ask "What do you most respect in a woman?". Or rather than asking "Are you clean and tidy?" you could ask "When did you last clean your bath?"

Questions that involve a choice between two things can also be good fun and very revealing. For example, you could ask "If you had to be outside or inside all day every day, which would you pick?" or "If you had to choose between physical appearance and intelligence for your next partner, which would you pick?"

---

[28] If you haven't already purchased my 150 dating questions, a second date is the perfect time to use them. Visit rachelnewdatingcoach.co.uk/purchase

Response

3. Questions to ask to check on red flags over the first few dates:

    - Do they show an interest in you as a person rather than referring to your appearance or talking about themselves too much?
    - Do they engage in a proper conversation, back and forth?
    - Are they getting emotionally involved too quickly?
    - Do they get intimate online or pressurise you to do so?
    - Do they disappear for ages then reappear sporadically in the messaging?
    - Do they follow up and ask how things went e.g. if you've had a bad day/are ill/had something important on?
    - Are they keen one minute and distant the next?
    - Do they show empathy?
    - Do they talk about friends and family or do they seem to be a loner?
    - Do they ever phone you? Are you encouraged to phone them?
    - Do they get angry or upset?
    - Do you have misunderstandings?
    - Do they treat waiters/waitresses etc well?
    - Do they make eye contact and stay focused on you?
    - Do they have any social media accounts and do they show you pictures from them?
    - Do they invite you to their home?
    - Do they criticise you or others a lot?
    - Are they very up and down in their moods?
    - Do they become very irrational/angry when you disagree?
    - Do they remember your name and other details?
    - Do they ask you for money?[29]

4. Make a list of what you want to find out on the second date. This should include some follow-ups from the first date on anything you want to find out more about.

---

[29] rachelnewdatingcoach.co.uk/2017/05/19/could-i-be-the-victim-of-a-dating-scam

5. Write down what you want from the date and what your policy is on kissing and other forms of intimacy, so that you have decided in advance what is right for you and feel confident about that.

When should I become intimate?

Reflection

1. Imagine you are on your tenth date with someone. When looking back at the first few dates, what would you like your memories to be of the way things progressed physically?

2. How would things be different if you waited more or less time to become intimate?[30]

3. How have your attitudes towards intimacy changed since COVID?

Discussion

Decide in advance when you want to become sexually intimate. Each time you meet you will find out more, and need to digest the information. So it is best not to make the decision while actually on a date.

Pre-COVID, many people kissed by the third date. If you are not ready, but are still interested, it might be a good idea to communicate this to the other person, to avoid misunderstanding. You might want to check if they are dating other people and decide how you feel about the possibility of them kissing more than one person in a limited time frame. For example, you may think it is wise to have a ten day gap between kissing one person and another, because of the risks of COVID.

You may both also want to see proof of COVID vaccinations from an early stage. Don't let yourself become intimated into not being cautious and sensible. Decide in advance what your deal-breakers are here and don't compromise.

---

[30] Read and reflect on rachelnewdatingcoach.co.uk/2016/11/28/when-should-you-sleep-with-your-date

Beginning to become intimate could just mean kissing and cuddling in the park or on the sofa. There is no rush.

When you are ready to become intimate, you may want to check on whether they are dating other people, whether they have other sexual partners (and if so, whether they have their consent to be in an open relationship).

At some point you should discuss their practices of using protection and getting checked for sexually transmitted infections (STIs). However, many people will use condoms the first few times they have intercourse without this discussion. (Do note that condoms do not prevent all STIs. Do your research.) They may then agree to become exclusive, get tested and then choose not to use condoms (while still protecting against pregnancy where this is a possibility).

When you decide to visit their home, or you invite them to your home and live alone, make sure a friend knows where you are and check in with them regularly.[31]

Decide what you will do if you arrive and their home is too unclean, untidy or unsuitable or you feel uncomfortable. Make sure you have the ability to order a taxi immediately if needed. Your phone should be fully charged before you go on your date and you should have both cash and bank cards with you.

You also need to make it clear before you agree to be alone with them that you are NOT consenting to be sexually intimate. You have every right to make decisions as you go along and say when you don't feel comfortable. Similarly, you must ask for consent a number of times as things develop. Consent to one thing does not imply consent to another.[32]

---

[31] rachelnewdatingcoach.co.uk/2017/10/09/protecting-yourself-from-online-dating-crime

[32] The Cup of Tea Consent video is essential viewing: https://www.youtube.com/watch?v=pZwvrxVavnQ

You should not assume that staying the night is a pre-requisite to being intimate. Discuss this and don't be offended if the other person isn't comfortable with it the first few times. They may need their space or have other things planned for the next morning. Make sure you have a plan to get home or a way to gently ask them to leave.

> "Love consists of this: two solitudes that meet, protect and greet each other."
>
> Rainer Maria Rilke, 1875-1926

On the other hand, if things are going well inviting them to stay over is a warm and human way to treat someone after intimacy, when you may both be feeling more vulnerable to each other. Don't stretch things out too long the next day, though. Perhaps have a leisurely breakfast or go for a short walk or a coffee, and then say goodbye. Less is more!

Response

Being assertive about your expectations and standards is an indirect way of communicating the respect you have for yourself and what you deserve. If you are finding it difficult to feel confident about asking these questions and saying what you feel comfortable with, you may need to revisit the earliest sections of this book. Don't allow anyone to make you feel bad or guilty about your needs or to undermine your standards.

How should the first ten dates look?

Reflection

1. How often would you like to see your date?

2. How could you interpret it if they wanted to see you more or less often than you expected?

3. Make a list of a range of different activities you'd like to try in the first ten dates, to get a good feel for how your date is in different situations.

4. What would you hope to know after ten dates about the way things were going?

Discussion

Circumstances and personality differences may dictate the pace of dating. Some people need more space than others.[33] You may have to adapt to someone else's needs and not interpret it as meaning they are less keen. The same applies to communicating in between dates. Some like to keep in touch every day, others prefer not to.

> "Love one another but make not a bond of love: let it rather be a moving sea between the shores of your souls"
>
> Kahlil Gibran, *The Prophet,* 1923

If you are seeing each other once or twice a week, ten dates should take you to roughly the two or three month mark. By that stage, most people have stayed over at each other's homes and spent a few hours in the daytime together. You are likely to have cooked for each other but not to have left a toothbrush in the bathroom yet.

---

[33] rachelnewdatingcoach.co.uk/2019/11/13/needing-space

You won't be at the stage of calling it a relationship. You might not have met any family or friends yet, but this is a good next stage. Seeing how they relate to others is a really important test. When introducing each other, just use your names – no need to worry about using words like "boyfriend" at the moment.

Response

Keep a journal or talk to friends regularly about how it's going and what you learn about them. (Pick friends whose judgment you trust.) As time goes on, you will inevitably find out some ways in which you are not compatible or in which they are challenging, and they will for you. This is normal. No two people can be perfectly matched on everything. But you'll have to keep reassessing whether the costs outweigh the benefits, and deciding what you can put up with.

For each challenge, ask yourself what the effects are on you and what it tells you about their values and lifestyle. Try not to react just because it's something they do differently from you – keep an open mind when possible. For example, you may like to plan everything in advance and they may prefer to be spontaneous. The two approaches both have their advantages and disadvantages. You can adapt to each other, taking turns to be responsible for the date and learning to laugh at your differences rather than turning it into a source of tension or competition.

How do I move into a relationship?

Reflection

1. What images, words and emotions does the word "relationship" conjure up for you? How is it different from dating?

2. How, for you, is a relationship at say six months different from one at six years?

3. Discuss these questions with your date and friends to get different answers and perspectives.

4. Ask your date what they like about you and what they value about the time you spend together. Ask yourself the same questions.

5. Imagine what life would be like without them around. What would be better, what would be worse, and what would just be different? How would you feel?

Discussion

Everyone is different about the timescale for moving from dating into a relationship. Most people have a conversation about where things are heading somewhere between two and six months, with three to four months being the most common. Sometimes it is triggered by an imminent meeting with each other's friends and family, or a holiday like Christmas, where you need to decide how much time to spend together.

Although it usually comes up naturally, you may want to prepare what to say. You can ask a question like "So, are things between us still interesting for you?" or "What do you think we'll be doing in three months' time?" or "Are you happy with how things are between us?" This can get the conversation started, and then you can be more direct as you feel it develops, asking something like "So I've just been telling people we're dating, but I'm wondering if we are moving towards calling it a relationship?"

If they're not ready for this, it doesn't necessarily mean things won't work out. Try to find out more about how they're feeling, whether they have a fear of commitment or trust, whether it's circumstances, worries about family disapproval, or whatever. Then you can discuss it again in a month or two.

However, you may feel that they are just not seeing things in the same way as you. You may be looking for something serious but they are not, or vice versa. Many people look back and wish they'd ended things at the three month mark. Try to be objective about what you want and realistic about whether this relationship can meet your needs.

You may also find yourself getting swamped by their needs and realising the relationship is unbalanced. You can't be their saviour and it's unlikely that you can change them. How much you both put into and get out of the relationship needs to be sustainable. Discussing this with a dating or relationships coach can be very helpful at this stage.

It's important to accept that not everything will go according to the ideal timescale. There will likely be at least one unexpected life event at a premature time. Perhaps one of you will have a birthday really soon after you start dating; or wonder whether to invite the other to a funeral or wedding; or spend a long period of time apart on a holiday or for work. You will need to discuss and judge on each case how to support each other without scaring each other off. If possible, keep presents small, avoid relationship responsibilities too early, and don't spend too much time together.

Response

6. Before having the conversation about calling it a relationship, take time to journal or talk to someone about your dating experiences. Don't brush under the carpet issues and emotions that need to be aired and acknowledged.

7. Assess how accommodating or demanding you are being in the relationship and whether this needs to be adjusted. We all tend to swing to one extreme or the other, depending on our history. Are you repeating patterns against or reacting from previous relationships, whether romantic or family? This is a huge area that may need unpicking with help.

How do I know someone is right for me?

Reflection

On each date, ask yourselves:

1. Do we bring out the best in each other?
2. Can we be ourselves with each other?
3. Do we respect each other?
4. Do we feel secure about our relationship through the way we communicate with each other, both in person and when apart?
5. Are we both emotionally available and able to show empathy and sensitivity?[34]
6. Do we feel at ease with each other's sense of humour?
7. Do we feel comfortable and proud introducing each other to our family and friends?
8. How do we argue with each other? Are we good at apologising?
9. Are our lives moving in similar directions?
10. Do our activities together reflect shared values and goals?
11. Is there a good balance between giving and receiving?
12. Are we satisfied with our sexual connection? Are we both able to express ourselves and our needs?

---

[34] rachelnewdatingcoach.co.uk/2017/01/09/am-i-emotionally-available

Discussion

It takes time to discover everything you need to know about someone. It may be six months in before you discover they have very different views about politics from you, or clean their bathroom much less often than you, or never remember their Mum's birthday, or are much more obsessed with football than you realised. You can't speed the process up or have an exhaustive check-list because we all have unique ways of being different from each other. And then there are all the things they will discover about you!

We are also on our best behaviour for the first few months, displaying our ideal self. Being in a new relationship gives us the chance to behave differently from previous relationships and break old patterns such as how we argue or apologise,[35] but they are not always sustainable, especially when we are stressed or multi-tasking.

On the other hand, it is important that you are both able to keep the novelty and interest going, appreciating each other and continuing to plan unusual and fun dates.

"Never love anyone who treats you like you're ordinary."
Oscar Wilde, 1854-1900

The more you can talk about your answers to the questions above, the better for the health of your relationship.

Relationships are most likely to succeed when both parties have good relationship skills, even if they are not especially compatible. More of this in the next section.

---

[35] rachelnewdatingcoach.co.uk/2017/03/10/the-s-word-saying-sorry-to-your-date

Response

13. Think about what you are bringing to the relationship. Are there ways in which you can do more to bring out the best in each other?

14. Notice how you both behave when you ask each other to do something differently. Are you asking in a constructive way, picking the right time and getting a balance of positive to negative? Are you responding defensively or being flexible? How could you both improve?

15. Keep talking about your relationship skills with each other and working on ways to make things even better.

What makes a good relationship?

Reflection

Even if you are very compatible, unless you have key relationship skills, thing can be challenging. These include the following. Assess yourselves on each skill, with 1 for "rarely" to 5 for "very often":

1. We can listen to each other.

2. We respond warmly to each other.

3. We can be light-hearted about our differences and accept them.

4. We focus on the positives.

5. We give each other praise and appreciation.[36]

6. We can back down and change our minds.

7. We are open-minded to each other's perspectives.

8. We compromise in ways that are equally empowering to both of us.

9. We communicate about our emotions.

10. We are aware of each other's trigger points and how to support each other.

11. We can argue without hurting each other and have ways to repair the breach.[37]

12. We agree on the nature of our relationship and its direction and purpose.

---

[36] rachelnewdatingcoach.co.uk/2020/06/08/appreciating-your-partner-without-being-cheesy

[37] These questions are based on the relationship skills in *The Seven Principles For Making Marriage Work* by John and Nan Gottman.

13. We both have equal power and freedom.

14. We both feel safe and secure and trust each other.

15. We are both happy with our levels of dependence and independence.

Discussion

Unless you are a relationship expert. you have probably scored low on quite a few of the above. Even if you have had several long-term relationships before, you will no doubt find areas for improvement. The journey towards better relationships never ends as we learn more about each other and our relationship dynamic every day.

Relationships, like plants, need regular nourishment, and working at these skills is essential for your relationship to succeed. Just as we wouldn't try to fly a plane or teach children without education and training, we need relationship training and we need time to reflect.

To mix the metaphors, it is also important to keep fanning the flame of excitement, novelty, passion and mystery, and not to let things become routine and predictable.[38]

Developing an optimistic, positive approach to life as well as your relationship rather than focusing on the negative is essential. Your perceptions are better predictors of your relationship satisfaction than your personality.[39]

However, it is important to remember that a good relationship doesn't have to last forever. Sometimes it can come to a natural end without it being a failure. We may have different directions we want to go in and our needs can change. This means you don't have to imagine being together for the rest of your lives in order to decide whether to be in a relationship with someone or to judge your relationship as good.

---

[38] For more on this, read Mating in Captivity by couples therapist, Esther Perel.

[39] Joel, S. (2020). Machine learning uncovers the most robust self-report predictors of relationship quality across 43 longitudinal couples studies. *Proceedings of the National Academy of Sciences, 117* (32), 19061-19071.

Response

16. Don't wait for things to go wrong before addressing these key skills. Start work on them, one at a time, perhaps with the help of a relationship coach or counsellor.

17. You might want to read *The Seven Principles For Making Marriage Work* by John and Nan Gottman, which is based on extensive evidence from couples whose relationships both succeeded and failed, and the effect of their therapeutic tools.

18. Set aside time each week to think, reflect, write and talk about your relationship.

19. Spend time with other people who have good relationships and learn from them. Avoid people in dysfunctional relationships if possible so you are feeding your mind with good role models and norms. The same applies to what you read, watch and listen to.

Conclusion

If you have got the most from this workbook, you will have journeyed through the whole dating process, from knowing who you are, to deciding on your relationship needs, to meeting lots of interesting people, to finding a relationship. You will have invested time in making notes, reflecting and discussing with others or your coach. You should feel more self-aware, comfortable and happy with yourself, and able

Here are some final thoughts about getting the best out of all our relationships - whether a romantic partner, a date, family, friends, children or work colleagues.

In all our relationships, there needs to be a balance between making things happen and not being controlling, between being proactive and letting go. It can be hard to strike that middle ground, and it can alter minute by minute. You may decide to let one thing slide but ask for change on another. You may both tend towards one or the other end of the control scale. It's something you'll need to keep assessing and adjusting throughout your life.

One vital ingredient is to relate to others in a relaxed, loving way with a light touch. That means you must both care for your inner lives separately as well as together. You will relate to each other much more productively if you like yourself and are not overwhelmed by daily life.

Humour, emotional and physical warmth, appreciation and tolerance can also smooth the path. Creating this positivity for your relationship on a daily basis builds up "credit" in advance of challenges or favours needed. It also prepares you for a romantic relationship if you are already developing these skills in other areas of your life.

For those who are still dating, don't give up hope. Remember the research about growth versus loss mindsets and keep focusing on the gains and opportunities. There will come a day when you look back at this time – will you wish you'd enjoyed your dating days more?

This quotation is often attributed to Einstein: "Insanity is doing the same thing over and over and expecting different results." If your efforts aren't working, get some help from someone neutral and objective, such as a dating coach. In these post-pandemic times, we are more able than ever to ask for support for others in all areas of our lives, including our relationships.

Ultimately, my motivation for helping you and guiding you through your journey is to provide you with a way to live that makes you happy, safe and secure, but also frees you to find ways to make some kind of positive difference to others, both in your personal and professional lives.

Being loved allows you to love others, and developing relationship skills and a good self-image will let you do this without using up all your emotional resources.

"When we love, we always strive to become better than we are. When we strive to become better than we are, everything around us becomes better too."

Paulo Coelho, The Alchemist, 1988

Rachel New

2021

Further reading

The Course of Love by Alain de Botton. An insightful story of a contemporary relationship with all the underlying psychological processes explained.

The Future of Seduction by Mia Levitin (2021). A great summary of everything about contemporary dating.

The Seven Principles for Making Marriage Work by John Gottman and Nan Silver. Evidence-based clinical psychologists share what predicts the success or failure of long-term relationships, with lots of practical tasks and real-life stories.

Mating in Captivity: How to keep desire and passion alive in long-term relationships by Esther Perel. This best-selling author and relationship therapist addresses our conflicting needs for intimacy and independence.

The Heartfix: An Online Dating Diary by Stella Grey. A compelling and honest account of 693 days of middle-aged dating.

How to choose a partner by Susan Quilliam. A relationship therapist takes you on a journey of self-discovery to work out what kind of relationship you want.

Labor of Love by Moira Weigel. The history of dating.

Come as You Are: The Surprising New Science That Will Transform Your Sex Life by Emily Nagoski. This award-winning 2017 book demystifies the science of female desire.

Great Sex Starts at 50 by Tracey Cox. Practical advice and information about the menopause and changes to the body and relationships, for all sexualities and genders.

How to Understand Your Sexuality : A Practical Guide for Exploring Who You are by Meg-John Barker and Alex Iantaffi. With a new edition for 2021, this is down-to-earth guide to sexuality and how it links to our identities, desires, personal experiences and the world around us. It includes activities and reflection tasks.

Queer Sex: A Trans and Non-Binary Guide to Intimacy, Pleasure and Relationships by Juno Roche. A clear and honest guide that everyone can read to broaden your understanding of how gender has an impact on sexual relations, as well as being a great resource for the trans and non-binary community. Longlisted for the Polari First Book Prize 2019.

Queenie by Candice-Carty Williams. A poignant and hilarious novel about the brutal realities of dating as a Black woman in London. British Book Award winner 2020.

Heartburn by Nora Ephron. An emotionally honest novel about a psychotherapist coming to terms with her own relationship problems.

Rachel New is a Dating and Relationships Coach based in London, UK. She is also qualified as a teacher, life and mindfulness coach, and has a Masters in psychology.

To find out more, join a workshop, contact her or sign up for her latest blog posts, visit

www.rachelnewdatingcoach.co.uk

Facebook: @rachelnewdatingcoach

Twitter: @RNewDatingCoach

Instagram: @racheldatingadvice

YouTube: Rachel New Dating Coach

If you found this book useful, please support Rachel by reviewing it on Amazon.

Your Notes

Printed in Great Britain
by Amazon